Autism – Parents' Guide to Autism Spectrum Disorder

The following eBook is reproduced below with the goal of providing information that is as accurate and reliable as possible. Regardless, purchasing this eBook can be seen as consent to the fact that both the publisher and the author of this book are in no way experts on the topics discussed within and that any recommendations or suggestions that are made herein are for entertainment purposes only. Professionals should be consulted as needed prior to undertaking any of the action endorsed herein.

This declaration is deemed fair and valid by both the American Bar Association and the Committee of Publishers Association and is legally binding throughout the United States.

Furthermore, the transmission, duplication, or reproduction of any of the following work including specific information will be considered an illegal act irrespective of if it is done electronically or in print. This extends to creating a secondary or tertiary copy of the work or a recorded copy and is only allowed with the express written consent from the Publisher. All additional rights reserved.

The information in the following pages is broadly considered a truthful and accurate account of facts and as such, any inattention, use, or misuse of the information in question by the reader will render any resulting actions solely under their purview. There are no scenarios in which the publisher or the original author of this work can be in any fashion deemed liable for any hardship or damages that may befall them after undertaking information described herein.

Additionally, the information in the following pages is intended only for informational purposes and should thus be thought of as universal. As befitting its nature, it is presented without assurance regarding its prolonged validity or interim quality. Trademarks that are mentioned are done without written consent and can in no way be considered an endorsement from the trademark holder.

Table of Contents

Introduction

Congratulations on downloading *Autism – Parents' Guide to Autism Spectrum Disorder* and thank you for doing so.

The following chapters will discuss the symptoms and characteristics that make up Autism Spectrum Disorder and will give information on various aspects of parenting a child with Autism Spectrum Disorder.

There are plenty of books on this subject on the market, so thanks again for choosing this one! Every effort was made to ensure it is full of as much useful information as possible. Please enjoy!

BONUS:

As a way of saying thank you for purchasing my book, please use your link below to claim your free ebook

I have laid down Top 10 Tips Guide for you to Overcoming Obsessions and Compulsions Using Mindfulness

https://bit.ly/2TDMNkn

You can also share your link with your friends and families whom you think that can benefit from the guide or you can forward them the link as a gift!

Chapter 1: Introduction to Autism

The word "Autism" can refer to a few different things. It can describe a symptom, a disorder, and a syndrome. The idea for the conception of autism that we currently have is based on a negative social effect. The term "autistic isolation" comes from the description of psychiatric patients who had kept socially isolated.

Let's discuss autism as a disorder. Autism Spectrum Disorder (the most current nomenclature for the disorder) can be considered a developmental disorder, characterized by impairments in communication and social relationships. It is a quite complex disorder. It involves delays and problems in a range of emotional, cognitive, motor and sensory abilities. The specific behaviors that might come from the diagnosis are not specific to autism, and rather come from a fundamental problem in relating, communicating, and thinking. These behaviors could be bodily spinning, perseverating on a specific word without apparent meaning, lining up toys, or other behaviors.

The behavioral characteristics involve repetitive and restrictive patterns of behavior, with the onset of these patterns before the age of three. So, the combinations of both the impairment in relational functioning along with repetitive, restrictive, or stereotyped patterns of behavior make up the "what" of autism spectrum disorder.

This disorder has attracted more and more attention for the last twenty or so years. The attention has manifested itself in books, research publications, blogs, and other forms of media. As the awareness of the disorder has increased, so has research. The first mentions of autism came way back in the 1960s, but by most standards, autism is a relatively new and misunderstood condition. It is a modern disorder and is known through the current cultural and technological lens in which we live. It has become known as a result of atypical development and also seems to have some environmental causes.

Autism has been treated in various ways; it has been treated as a psychological, neurological, behavioral, and genetic disorder. Leo Kanner, a psychologist well known for writing about autism, leaned toward an organic interpretation. He theorized that it was caused by inherent differences in the brains of the children. His writing leaves the category ultimately open to interpretation, however

The cause of autism spectrum disorder is still unknown. Some of the research supports the idea that ASD can come from genetic influences. Identical twins are more likely to both have the disorder than are fraternal twins. There are other factors that have been shown to have an influence as well. These include the immunological, metabolic, and environmental factors in a child's life. No single cause has been definitively shown to produce the disorder. A helpful way to think about the underlying cause of autism is to think about it in terms of cumulative risk. This helps to recognize that many factors interact to cause the disorder. Factors related to the prenatal experience may make a child vulnerable to challenges early on, including stress, illness. This is a new way to think about causation that recognizes that there is some genetic influence, but that sees the gradual emergence of problems over time, and recognizes that there can be a developmental pathway for the child.

Autism and ASD presents a wide variety of problems, and with them, a variety of severity. Most of the time, these conditions will cause difficulty in relating and forming relationships, communicating, and thinking. They are very complicated developmental problems. The problems can appear differently and in different combinations. For example, children with what used to be called Asperger's syndrome often have big vocabularies and can be early readers. However, they have trouble using words in a meaningful way. They might have trouble using them with emotional relevance. They may repeat words over and over or understand only the strictest definition of the word.

Another variation that comes up is motor planning problems. Some children have trouble moving their tongue and the muscles in their mouths to help them speak. They may appear to have cognitive disabilities when they simply have trouble with the physical limitations of their moral-motor skills.

There are a few basic problems that tend to characterize autism and ASD. One involves intimacy and warmth. If a child has a problem in this area, the child may find it difficult to seek out adults they are really comfortable with. Another is communication. If the child is not engaging in a consistent flow of emotional signaling with smiles, frowns, head nods, and other physical gestures, they may be having problems in this area. The third is language and the use of language. If a child is having problems in this area, the words or symbols may lack emotional investment or desire.

Chapter 2: Understanding Child Autistic?

In order to understand a child with ASD, a parent must strive for engagement. Engagement can be small, a physical gesture or habit of touch, or a verbal exchange. By engaging, the parent will be able to try and enter the child's world. Once the parent has entered the child's world, they can help her enter into a shared world with others. At the core deficits of autism are difficulty with attention and with engagement, this can become the first goal for parents, educators, and other professionals working with children with ASD.

Parents are the constant in the lives of children with ASD. They are the people who will be with them as they grow through the developmental stages. They will see their child face challenges, achieve success, and struggle with navigating life just as all of us do. Likewise, the presence of an autism spectrum disorder is also a constant in the life of the parents and family. The mystery of autism can be challenging for families who come into contact with children who have it. Families of children with ASD will need to know their children well. They will also find themselves having to communicate about the disorder to other parents and members of the community.

First of all, parents should recognize and celebrate a child's individuality and uniqueness, rather than focusing on the child's symptoms and the difficulties that ASD can provide. The individuality and uniqueness of what is most rewarding to everyone who is working with the child. It is important that professionals listen to parents talk about their children's positive traits.

When the symptoms of ASD start to emerge around age 2 and 3, parents might feel like things are a little "off." There may be a lack of smiling or crying or a troubling lack of development in communication. The most severe cases of ASD will b noticed earliest. The early marker for this is usually a problem with speech or communication. This can make parents frustrated that they are not able to share communication with their children. Sometimes, the early signs can include unusual behavior with toys or people. The child may not be able to engage with play using toys as a child typically world. They may have habits of walking around or focusing on a certain aspect of the world.

In other cases, the parents may not notice symptoms until the child has to be in an environment with other children. Some parents recall seeing their children with AD very unhappy and uncomfortable when first starting school.

Parents will also notice sensitivities to sensory stimuli- sounds, touch, and foods. At first, these can be seen as peculiar quirks of the child, but eventually will contribute to problems in the child's development.

Parents look toward the future with hope when a child is born. They have the desire to protect, nurture, and love their children so that they can reach adulthood and have a good life. Some parents will feel very threatened when ASD is presented. They may feel that they have failed in their risk of protection, the ability of the child to succeed is compromised, and the parent-child relationship must be redefined. It makes sense that a parent might feel fear and anxiety when facing the potential diagnosis of autism or ASD. The early stages of diagnosis may be a time of great struggle for parents; they may experience a sense of dislocation. Before the diagnosis, they had a set of ideas, hopes, and goals for the child. After the diagnosis, they have to adjust their expectations and orientation to the current level of reality. They may feel isolated from friends and family who have not had the experience of dealing with ASD like they have. Other members of extended family may resist accepting the situation, and may even blame the parents.

One way to reconcile this difficult time is to acknowledge that autism and ASD is a mystery and unsolved mysteries are difficult to deal with Parents may need to address a feeling of helplessness and realize that they are not alone in their confusion. Parents that are able to do this will be able to begin the process of active coping and redefine their goals for the child.

In order to readjust their goals for their child and start to help the child on their developmental journey, a parent must identify and acknowledge the child's strengths and weaknesses. Kids with ASD may often have exceptional ability in one isolated area and have a hard time in other aspects of functioning. Here's an example of a child with ASD who has an unpredictable balance of strengths and weaknesses: A four-year-old child, Alison, had very limited speech at her initial evaluation and could only approximate the word "Fire truck" by saying "ee-awk."

This same child had been spelling "fire truck" with magnetic letters on the refrigerator since the age of 2. Understanding your kids' strengths and weaknesses can be challenging because children with ASD don't respond to testing situations in ways that you would think. They don't pay attention to what they are there to do, or talk with the test facilitator, preferring to use their papers and pencils in unlikely ways or fidgeting in their chair. Getting to know a child with ASD is an art.

As the child reaches the age of differentiation, starting to understand the difference between self and others, they will start to learn to integrate a sense of self. An integrated self is able to interact with the integrated sense of another. Children at this age use patterns to see how the world worlds. Turning a doorknob opens the door. Knocking over this object makes a loud noise. Children start to see the world in patterns and increase their understanding of how it works. This leads to expectations of the world and mastery of tasks and physicality. They will start to be able to tell approval apart from disapproval, and acceptance from rejection. They will start to utilize their awareness to respond differently.

Children with ASD may have difficulty making inferences, empathizing with others, and dealing with other people's emotions. Parents should have empathy for their kids around this time and recognize that their lack of emotional signaling does not signify a lack of love.

Chapter 3: Diagnosis of the Condition

The diagnosis of ASD can be difficult. There is no medical test, like a blood test, to look for the presence of ASD. Doctors will require observation of the child's behavior, interaction, and development to make a firm diagnosis. Sometimes the diagnosis can come at around 18 months or even earlier. By the time the child is 2, however, a diagnosis by a trusted professional can be considered reliable. Many circumstances lead to a child not receiving a diagnosis of ASD until they are much older than 2 or 3. This might lead to a lack of the crucial early developmental help that the child needs.

The first step in the process of diagnosis for ASD is a developmental screening. This consists of a brief test around learning skills, to detect delays in education or cognitive development. During this test, the professional who is administering the test may ask the parents questions about their experience living with the child. They might interact or even play with the child to observe the child's physicality, affect, and communication. Children should generally be screened for delays in the above areas at the ages of 9 months, 18 months, and 24 months. Additional screening is usually okay and could be necessary if the child has experienced conditions that lead to a higher risk of developmental problems.

The next step in the diagnosis of ASD would be a more comprehensive evaluation of the child's development and behavior. This may also include a lengthier interview with the parents. The child's vision and hearing will be inspected, and some other genetic or neurological testing may occur. In some cases, the primary care doctor will elect to refer the family to a specialist. Some specialist's titles include Developmental Pediatrician, Child Neurologists, and Child Psychologists.

In this comprehensive development, the professional providing care will look for numerous aspects of observable signs of ASD and look to characterize that particular child's idiosyncratic condition. They will identify the problems with communication, behavior, or social skills that the child may be specifically dealing with. They may also be responsible for evaluating the parent's level of stress and determine what the parent needs to raise their child productively and healthily.

There have been multiple studies that looked at the reliability of information provided by parents about their children's development. The research has indicated that parents are pretty good at describing their children and that incorporating the parent into the diagnosis process can help communication among the family, increase the doctor's awareness, and provide a clearer picture of the problems.

The diagnosis process can provide parents and children an idea of what to come. Once they have an idea of what is coming for their child, they can begin to bolster their development, build a closer relationship, and monitor their child's developmental process.

Chapter 4: The Sensory, Social Interaction, and Thinking Pattern

Everyone is unique in the way they experience the world through their senses. By paying attention to the unique differences in children with ASD, we can help them to become more flexible and to develop more fully.

The way that individuals with ASD experience the world through their senses is affected by all of the previously discussed factors that are considered to be part of the cause of ASD. These include genetic, prenatal, and postnatal factors. These influences tend to express themselves in the way that children react to sensations, organize movement, and process and comprehend what they hear and see. Working with children with ASD requires us to remember to take into account their "unique biologies."

All children are born with sensory and motor systems, but these systems need to be working together and coordinating in the right way. The thing that helps those sensory and motor patterns connect at a higher level is emotion. A child's sensations get connected to her actions through her emotions. For example, when a baby turns to look at her mother, she is doing so in part because the mother's voice is a pleasurable sensation.

If the baby is hypersensitive to sound, however, the normal volume for a voice may be upsetting. You can see how this could cause difficulties coordinating the senses and motor patterns. It will cause the child to have trouble connecting with the mother. The over-stimulation may lead to a panic by the child. Likewise, if the child is not able to hear her mother or father calling to her, she may have a difficult time looking at her parents, which would've been guided by the sound of the voice. She may look off to the other direction and experience a lack to exchange of smiles and learns not to look for warm connections.

Auditory processing is how we hear information and how we comprehend what we hear. There is a coding system that helps us discriminate between different sounds, such as high or low pitch, and to make sense of sounds regarding words and language. Language requires auditory processing and expressing thoughts and responses to others. Often times, children with ASD run into problems in the area of expressive language. Sometimes they can't make sense of the information that they are receiving. Sometimes they can't express what's going on in their heads. Some will have difficulty with both.

Problems with auditory processing can lead to problems in other areas. One example would be a child with ASD who is having aggressive behaviors in the classroom. At first, it appears that the problem is that the child is purposely aggressive for no reason. However, if the caregivers or professionals working with the child look a little closer, they may realize that the child has difficulty hearing instructions, and then becomes frustrated with the challenge of fitting in. This frustration can lead to aggressive behaviors, as the child expresses their anger for their situation. Sometimes, drawing can help a child complexly express their thinking without having to navigate the difficulties of language.

Another area, which can cause issues, is motor planning and sequencing. This refers to how we act on our ideas and thoughts, usually in response to something else. This is quite the process for young infants. First, they register the sound and must find it interesting. Then they have to find the physical ability to move their muscles (which they don't have much practice with_ so that they can turn their neck or body toward the sound. Finally, they have to enact the force to turn their body, coordinating the muscle movements so that they work as desired. They look for the person whose voice they have heard and try to locate the face from which it came. There are many more complex tasks that the infant will have to learn in the coming months.

After infancy, the child must learn to have purposeful movement, followed by an awareness of the body boundaries of self and other. They will learn to see how their body affects others in space and time, and how to use the body for coordination in their motor actions. Sometimes a child with ASD will reach for their mother's hand to do something, rather than using their own hand.

They may lack the awareness that they can hold and turn something. They had learned that their parents' hands could do it better and did not develop the skills required to use their own hands. A lot of work is needed to make up for this developmental deficiency. Things like music or games that engage the child in physical activity like clapping can encourage the child to use their hands in space and time. We can encourage them to lift off the top of a container to get something or to pull on the strings of a bow to open a package.

The area of vision and logical reasoning is another area to consider. Children often will try to use toys as if they are real, for example, trying to put on doll clothes or ride in a toy car. These experiments should not be discouraged; it is by trying things that we all learn. Sometimes children need to attempt to use toys illogically to move on to the phase of being able to use them as symbolic toys.

Simple tasks like helping to set a table can help a child to use their visual-logical reasoning and understand why things are the way they are.

Children at this stage will begin to draw some of the things they actually see, as they understand the level of object constancy and understanding that objects exist.

Children with ASD must learn to modulate their response to sensory stimuli. When they are feeling overwhelmed, it might feel like light is extremely bright, or that a voice is loud screeching. Some children with ASD under react to stimuli. They may barely recognize that you are there why you are talking to them or barely notice touch. This may cause kids to retreat and isolate because they don't feel any connection.

Therefore, the ability to modulate or regulate sensory input is a very challenging and important task for kids with AD. They may need to learn to amplify the necessary stimuli and learn coping skills to reduce their reactions to some stimuli.

Learning to reckon with typical social interaction will be an area of difficulty for most children with ASD. Communication is very important to anyone who is in contact with children with ASD. Once a child learns to pay attention to a caregiver and becomes calm and regulated, it is very critical for the child to learn to communicate meaningfully. It begins at the preverbal level, with gestures or nodding, or smiles or gurgling sounds. These provide the foundation for what will become words. The communication becomes exponentially faster throughout the child's early development.

Children will need to learn verbal skills to build on the pre-verbal level. First, they will need to master gestures. Children who don't develop gestures to develop language will have trouble responding to social signal, and will not know what to do and when to do it. The ability to use language also has an impact on cognition and intelligence. The fundamental principle of causality is learned when a child learns that they can get a smile from their mother by smiling, cooing, or making little gestures. If equal communication is not provided, the child might learn causality in a too-limited way. Cognitive skills tend to grow out of language and are also extensions of the preverbal communication in.

Many children with ASD will have a hard time engaging in mutual communication. To find out where to start and how to engage with the child, a professional will often try to observe the child interacting with others to see if the child is sharing their world or staying in it. They look to see if they can show the caregiver, even if they can't say, what they want. They will try to tell if the child can use gestures as a way to explore communicate.

The child must learn to be a two-way communicator. Often, the adult must improve their skills in communication. Sometimes a parent has room to improve in their physical gestures or language.

Let's discuss some of the ways that parents, caregivers, and professionals can encourage communication. First of all, it is important to follow the child's lead when possible. Tuning into the interests, emotions, and goals of the child is important for the child to feel a sense of purpose. Getting the child to exert their initiative and lead can be very therapeutic. The caregiver can take on the helper role, and assist the child as they choose their own actions and paths.

Let's say the child is dancing around the room. One way for the caregiver can meet the child where they are is by dancing with them. Reach out a hand, see if they assent, and now it's a two-way dance. For a different example, imagine a child who is continually playing with their own fingers in a self-stimulatory, obsessive way. This gives us a little bit of insight into their world. A caregiver may be able to use touch to stimulate the child's fingers to initiate communication. The child is focused on physical touch, so that becomes the entry point into helping them communicate. Another way of creating communication with the child is by being "playfully obstructive." IF the child is playing with a toy car, the caregiver might become the policeman who gets in the way of the child's car. This will provide the child with an opportunity to interact, and to play out a situation in which there is some emotional content.

There are a number of ways to get two-way communication going that involve games. Peek-a-boo games, hide-and-seek, music activities, and art activities are some examples. These can create a safe, structured environment for communication so that the child feels comfortable to do so.

The cognitive development and thinking patterns of children with ASD are highly idiosyncratic, and the uniqueness of each child should be carefully considered. Sometimes children with ASD are challenged at to low a rate. They aren't expected to advance much beyond the basics of engaging and communicating. However, children with ASD can progress well through all the stages of development. Once children separate reality from fantasy at a young age, they can progress to multicausal thinking. This is the ability to conceive of events as having multiple reasons. It is warm outside because the sun is in the sky and because it is summertime. Around this stage of development, children start giving more than one reason for events, and their cognitive abilities increase just the same. Another concept that is related to this ability is triangular thinking. This demonstrates the ability to understand a tripartite relationship by three separate entities.

In some stages of history, children with ASD were considered incapable of achieving higher levels of abstract and reflective thinking. We know now that may help children with ASD achieve incredible milestones and master them with depth and subtlety.

One of the important factors in learning and mastering thinking capacities is the way that they are interacted with in the home and at school and therapy. It is the job of teachers and parents to be firm and persistent but also to prevent themselves from falling into the habit of saying "that's bad" all the time and engendering all-or-nothing thinking. Abstract thinking will be a difficult achievement for all children. Children with ADS will need attention to achieve.

Chapter 5: How to Get the Attention of a Child with Autism

Parents have the ability to monitor their children, so they tend to have an intimate knowledge of the child's development. With this knowledge, they can spot the signs early and be able to respond adequately.

The first stage is to facilitate shared attention and regulation. For this, the parent will need to observe the baby's unique style of hearing, seeing, touching, smelling, and moving. Listen to see what kind of sounds are being responded to. It might be high pitches or low pitches. You can try slower rhythms and faster rhythms. See what kinds of touch the child enjoys to settle and comfortable.

Here's a strategy for navigating this stage: the "look and listen" game. The parent is face to face with the infant and tries to talk to him about his brown eyes, hair, and little nose. When doing this, the parent should try to keep their face animated and move it to the right and left, trying to capture the infant's attention for a few seconds. This game can be playing while holding the baby or you can have the infant seated. Another is the "soothe me" game. This involves rocking with the baby when they're fussy or tired. Soothingly touch the baby's head, arms, and so on, and gently move the toes and fingers in a "little piggy" type of game. Moving the child's arms, legs, fingers, and toes helps with sensory integration.

The next stage is facilitating engagement and relating. To help this stage, the parent should try to see what kinds of interactions bring the child pleasure. Peek-a-boo and hiding games that tend to delight most babies and rhythmic clapping games can help to integrate the auditory processing tasks. Troy to see when the child has a magic moment. This may happen when they are alert but relaxed, available and interacting. Follow the interests of the child, even if it is just silly noises. Instead of competing for attention with a toy, become part of the game. One activity that can be helpful with this is a simple smiling game. Use words and faces to entice the baby to use their facial expressions. Another is a dancing movement game. This is where you try to inspire the baby to make sounds and move around in rhythm with the voice. You might say, "Dance with me! I bet you can!"

The next stage is to facilitate purposeful emotional interactions. This involves a lot of animated facial expressions on the part of the caregiver. Sounds and gestures will be a part of this, as well as words and dramas. You can tell that the child is alert and enjoying the exchange by that twinkle in the eye. In this stage, it may be beneficial to treat all of the child's behavior, even it if is random, as purposeful. If she flaps her hands in excitement, you use it as the basis for an interactive dance move. If her play seems aimless as she pushes a car back and forth, you can announce that the there is a special delivery letter that tweeds to be carried in the car straight to a place that the child knows.

You can help your child do this by making his goals easier to achieve. You may move a toy closer to him after he points his finger. Then you can encourage the child's assertiveness by challenging him to do this, such as putting the teddy bear to bed at night. Here's an example of an activity that you can use here: look to see the child's facial expression and mirror these sounds and facial expressions back to the child in a playful way.

If you can evoke a response, you've created a very helpful line of development with a feedback loop. You can also try a circle-of-communication game. Try to see how many back-and-forth interactions you can sustain each time the baby does a predetermined physical goal, such as patting your head. See how many times they will try to open your hand when you've hidden something interesting inside. There is a circle of communication each time you go back and forth on any of these interactions.

The next stage of getting your child's attention and facilitating interaction is shared problem-solving. This will help to get the child solving problems in groups of other people. Create pretend-problems in play so that the child has a chance to play with problems. You might announce, "this car won't move! What are we going to do?" This will create a play barrier for the child with play goals. You can work up to a continuous flow of communication. It helps to have a very bright facial expression and show your feelings through your voice and expression to help the child clarify her intentions. This will increase the child's ability to plan movements, use the body and use senses and initiative skills in different circumstances.

Creating ideas is what comes after emotional interaction. This is where the child is challenged to express their needs, desires, and interests. The caregiver should create situations in which the child wants to express their feelings or intentions. They can use ideas both for imaginative play situations and in every day talking interactions. It is useful to combine words and ideas with effect in this stage. The child should be encouraged to use all types of idea or emotions or themes. The child needs to explore these areas in order to create their own ideas.   Parents can help the child to develop conversational skills by chitchatting. If the child is verbal, see how many circles of communication you can have using words, phrases, or short sentences. You can turn even a one-word response into a long chat. Engage the child's ability to pretend by initiating play. You can introduce drama or new plot twists in the child's play. Challenge them to play in different ways and switch around characters. If you can take on the role of the narrator, this can help you to summarize the actions of the child and encourage the child to move along in the story.

The next stage is to facilitate logical thinking. This will involve using all of the stages that have come before; it will require that the child close circles of communication, using ideas, both in play and everyday interactions. They will need to link ideas and subplots. They build bridges between ideas in this way. Pull back on track if they get confused or fragmented, and challenge them to be pointed in their thinking. Open-ended questions are important in this scenario. Some possibilities have to do with the here-and-now: "What are you feeling right now? What are we talking about?"

Chapter 6: How to Help Improve Their Obsessive Behavior

When attempting to help improve or modify a child's obsessive behavior, parents should want to start by building on the existing knowledge that they already have. Parents are often very sensitive to their children's' behavior and needs, but sometimes they are not aware of the extensive knowledge they have.

One way that parents adapt to cope with problematic situations are by changing up routines. For example, some parents find that giving the child their favorite toy at night; they will cry less during that initial bedtime stage. Others found that their child would eat ham and bread separately, but not as a sandwich. Others notice that when their child is doing the math they have trouble aligning the numbers, but they still get the right answers. The parents bought him graph paper with lines on it so that he can line up is numbers and present them nicely.

Parents can find solutions like these when they take into consideration the root of the behaviors that they are seeing. Often these behaviors are obsessive or perseverate, meaning that the child comes back again and again to enact the same behavior. Although parents find solutions to these situations, sometimes they don't take a broader view of the solutions or root of the problem. By developing a vocabulary for identifying and describing the obsessive behavior, parents can understand better how to deal with behaviors and help the child to adapt.

Sometimes obsessive behaviors are indication of increased agitation or stress. The child may be rubbing their ears, twisting hair, or clasping hands together. These can be signs of impending crisis. The parent should be careful not to overreact to these signs because they have already learned to predict what the kinds of signs mean.

Parents are usually pretty well informed about their child's preferences. They should honor these preferences as much as possible, for this will decrease the need for obsessive behavior on the part of the child. Effective rewards for children with ASD are very individualized. What works for one child will not work for many others. Parents must work to apply their knowledge of the child to create rewards and environments that are stimulating and rewarding for the child. Parents must also strive to not fall into self-blame or self-doubt and must trust their decision-making abilities.

Often times, children with ASD are engaging in challenging behavior because they need or want something that they are not able to get. Other times they are trying to avoid doing something that they don't want to do. This demonstrates that obsessive behaviors are often attempts by children with ASD to communicate. It is rare for children, even children with severe autism, to behave badly just to test the patience of others. It is more likely that children are using strategies that they have found through experience to help them cope with problems.

The problem may seem trivial at the outside level. For example, the child may want to watch his favorite movie for the fourth time that day, or they may want so badly to avoid brushing their teeth that they have a mild crisis. These minor desires can transform into major disruptions. The parents will want to anticipate the children's needs, providing them with alternative ways to communicate their needs, and rewarding children for using these more positive approaches. This will help to reduce difficult behavior. Most parents use these strategies and don't even know it.

When analyzing behavior, there is a system of four steps that can be applied to objectively observe what's going on. The first is identifying the situations in which obsessive behavior occurs. The second is recognizing the reasons for challenging behavior. The third is finding positive alternatives to the obsessive behavior. Finally, the parents should reward positive behavior. Parents can use these steps to solve problems as they come up. This will lend itself to more positive family interactions.

Some common situations in which obsessive behaviors cause disruptions are daily routine activities like dressing, bathing, etc., enjoyable activities, crowds of people, strangers, too many instructions at once, too many demands, lack of stimulation, or over-stimulation. Knowing this can help parents to determine the antecedents, or causes, of behaviors. This is an important skill for prints. They must learn to describe what happens just before the trouble. Sometimes, avoiding the situation is the best option. Obviously, this is not always practical, so there are many situations in which adaptations are necessary. When there is a situation that can't be avoided, parents must anticipate that situation and prepare for it.

The preparation may look different in different situations. Sometimes it involves distracting a child. If there are some nice bright flowers, you can try to turn the child's attention toward them for a while. Sometimes, just telling the child that something unexpected is going to happen and offering some advice on what to do can help the child handle the situation, especially for older children. These can be manifested as small reminders, such as reminding the child to bring their jacket when it is cold outside.

Things like self-hygiene and attending school and therapy are situations that cannot be avoided. The child must endure some situations. The family's overall well being is improved if the child with ASD sleeps through the night, is eating, bathing, and feeling generally well. This requires the child to go through the active action that is required to make all of these things happen.

Remember, children with ASD usually can't articulate their needs and don't learn in the conventional ways. They tend to experience their wants and needs as intense and immediate. A delay in time can seem intolerable. Parents must work toward breaking this cycle. Usually, they can identify what the child wants. This s the first step to solving the problem of obsessive behavior. This gives us a specific task: finding an adapted alternative that will serve the same function. Children with ASD do not intend to be unpleasant. They just know that they are upset because they need something that they are not getting. Often the obsessive behavior comes up because the child simply wants attention. In this case, it can be necessary to modulate attention and use attention as a reward for certain behaviors.

Ignoring is not usually effective, and can be harmful. Ignoring the need will not make it go away. Ignoring children with ASD does nothing to teach them about adapted ways of getting their needs met. Proactive teaching of such alternatives is the way to reduce or eliminate obsessive behaviors.

Chapter 7: How to Teach Your Autistic Child

Once the parent has learned how to predict the antecedents of obsessive behaviors, they can start to teach the child a practical and positive adaptive alternative to the obsessive behavior. They should be careful not to take it all on at once; usually, they should target a specific situation to teach alternative skills about those situations. Once parents have identified the teaching goal, they have to be careful not to let challenging behavior be effective in that situation. This can prove a challenge for many parents because all parents want to help their child to be happy.

However, if the child learns that having a tantrum will get them what they want, the learning process will stall, and their development will be stunted. Another difficult part of this problem is that teaching the child the alternative behaviors don't work right at the time of the behavior. Useful learning doesn't take place when people are upset. Instead, parents should look to arrange situations in which the obsessive behavior is likely to occur and then intervene to teach the alternative skill before the child gets too far into an emotional state.

When teaching children with ASD, caregivers and professionals should use a positive communication strategy. Children who have good languages skills can learn to say, "help, please. "Others can learn to make a sign for "help."

Nonverbal children can be taught to use visual information to communicate their basic needs. Learning must be very specific and concrete for children with ASD. A child who learns to ask for help in making the bed will usually not apply that strategy to get help with anything eel. However, once parents find a way to teach the child to ask for help in one situation, such as using making the bed, they can teach the child to ask for help in other situations.

In historical and often outdated books on autism, there often is an image of children that are out of control, running around aimlessly and physically out-of-order. The idea used to be that children with ASD are self-absorbed, self-simulator, and couldn't relate at all with others. This is not the reality. Many children with ASD didn't show extreme behaviors and weren't even diagnosed. They were thought to be hard to educated because their behaviors were untreated and nobody understood their challenges. We have a new way of thinking about education in ASD now because we have seen the complex differences in children with ASD and better understand the signs, symptoms, and characteristics of the disorder.

Thinking can be difficult for children with ASD or other learning disabilities. Ti can be harder if they are only encouraged to regurgitate memorized facts. They can, however, learn to think with an appropriate learning style.

At the start, it is very important for the child to be engaged in a one-on-one approach. This must be coordinated between home and school. The home and school plans must be part of the overall program, which means that teachers and parents must meet somewhat frequently to share insight about what is going on with the child. If a school decides not to let parents observe or help out in the classroom, or if parents don't share what is going on at home, the education of the child may be at risk of being at a substantially lower quality. It can also be very helpful for parents of children with ASD to meet each other regularly and talk about heir experiences.

Some specialists can be very important in the child's learning, such as speech pathologists, occupational therapist's or music therapists. Already we see how demanding being a parent of a child with ASD can be, as the parent is responsible for arranging a relationship with the educational system that parents of a neurotypical child may not have to deal with. Then, they will need to coordinated therapeutic treatment if necessary.

Music therapy has been shown to be particularly useful in a child with ASD's learning. Music has a temporal (time) aspect and also engages the auditory sense, the tactile senses, and the visual sense. Music is unique in that it combines all of these directions of stimulation and fuses them with emotional content. The emotional content can come from many different aspects of the music; the interaction with the music therapist can provide a sense of warmth and connection. The song may be about something that the child likes, like a food or activity. A music therapist can help integrate all of these sensory experiences into positive learning and development for the child. Singing can help with the motor planning involved with speech. Eye contact can be improved. Issues around emotional expression can be alleviated, as the child is allowed a way to have cathartic experiences.

Once the fundamentals of learning are mastered, the focus of education shifts to promoting creative and logical thinking Rather than focusing on a goal, such as putting on shoes, the child will need to think about why we put on shoes. Our special education system has been created through a top-down model in which we look at what older, neuro-typical children can do and then apply those goals to younger children. This has provided some blocks in the development of our special education. Ti has come to involve a good deal of superficial skill building.

In order to advance in their learning, children have to be able to think. Thinking skills precipitate reading comprehension, history, math, and the other studies that the child will be challenged with. Thinking skills also precipitate better behaviors. Once children can think about why things are and what they are, they will be able to figure out why they shouldn't push other children and why they have to share.

To promote creative and logical thinking, an educational environment needs to spend time on the foundation-building endeavors and then grow from there.

Creative thinking is an interesting subject. It can be fostered in many ways. Activities that promote creative use of ideas include play, drama, art, and music, or physical activities. One of the most effective of these activities is play. It can be very important that the caregiver or teacher gets on the floor to interact with the child. If they are able to get on the floor and play with the child, they bring themselves down to the level of the child, and this provides the child with a sense of equality, and the caregiver seems less like an authority and more like a trusted figure. The parent or caregiver should engage the child in a pretend drama, trying to make the drama as complicated as possible. Children should be encouraged to think symbolically early in life. The skills involved in pretend play amount to a way that children connect the abstract with the concrete. It allows them to make sense of their world, to think of themselves and others in different ways, and to explore possibilities.

Parents should try to create an inviting environment for symbolic play and let the child explore and find new ways to act and learn. It is important that the child is allowed to initiate the play based on their own interests and curiosity. The play area can have toys and props that are related to real life. Try to think about what the child enjoys when choosing toys. Children readily understand toys that represent the real world with ASD, and it can be helpful to use the toys that the child loves. They represent the child's deeper attachments and are symbols that can help decode what the child is feeling. They may love animals, trucks, trains, or certain foods. The important thing is to join with the child in their interest and help expand and deepen the ideas through your interactions. Toys can constitute a sort of language for children with ASD, and this allows them to learn within play. They may play with toys before they begin to speak. They might be using it to show you their interests and thoughts before they are able to use their words.

It is appropriate to encourage representation in the way that the child is using toys. Some figures or dolls could represent family members or friends. The child is more likely to be able to handle this representational nature with names from their own family before they accept a figure with an unknown name. The parent needs to get involved with the drama here and act out the character that works with the child's play. A fun way to do this is to give symbolic meaning to furniture or other objects that are in the environment. When the child climbs to the top of the sofa, a parent can pretend they are climbing a mountain, and when he comes down the slide, treat it as if they are sliding down into the ocean.

Overall, it can be beneficial to expand and elaborate n the child's ideas so that they get an idea of how to expand on creative ideas. Stories are an important part of communication and creativity, and to create a compelling story, we need to elaborate and explore. You can introduce reasoning in this way, by inserting practical reasons for the play characters to act in a certain way. You can expand the range of themes and emotions by exploring different types of emotions, including anger, sadness, joy, surprise, jealousy rivalry, power, revenge, friendship, loyalty, justice, and morality.

Drama helps to illustrate all of these emotions and experiences. If possible, a caregiver or parent can provide reflection on the ideas and feelings during the story and after the story is over. Discussing the themes and feeling of the child and getting them to elicit the point of the story can help them to develop skills of abstraction and determine the right and wrong in the story. Symbolic play and reflective conversation can become safe ways to practice, understand, and master the range of emotional experiences. They are building bridges between ideas and thoughts, abstract and reality.

To help a child with ASD learn, some structure in the daily routine can be necessary. Children with ASD have differences in the way they process information. Some time of the day should be spent in a one-on-one or small group straightening processing abilities. This includes the auditory, visual-spatial, motor planning, sequencing, and sensory modulation. Activities like dance sports, art, and drama are great when integrated into these foundational components. Goals should be set of the individual's learning by determining the current level of the child's ability and then creating the goal for the next level for the child to achieve.

Twenty-minute increments usually work pretty well as a time frame for the attention span that is available. Twenty minutes can be spent on the floor playing working on language arts, twenty minutes spent on visual processing, and twenty minutes spent on regulatory processing.

Another part of the day should be spent working on higher levels of thinking. This begins by introducing creativity and high affect situations around situations that are understandable to the child.

Another third of the day can focus on thinking-based academics, in the hope of applying the higher-level thinking skills to schoolwork that is geared to the child's thinking capacities.

When it comes to planning the education, schooling, and other services for a child with ASD, parents can find themselves overwhelmed. First, the family receives a diagnosis and a set of intervention recommendations. Then, they have to sort through the phase of determining what services are available and practical for them to be able to be involved in.

There are many opinions about successful treatment and education for autism spectrum disorders to be found online, in books, or conversations with other parents. The kinds of services that are offered to children with ASD vary widely across the US. Parents who are knowledgeable about what is available to them can make good decisions about what their child needs.

There is no single type of educational or therapeutic program that will work for all children. There is a huge range of difficulties experienced by individuals with ASD, and the areas of strength are very uneven. The learning patterns are different in every child. This variability is one of the most challenging aspects of education for children n with ASD. Each experience the child has with the parent is unique. Individualization is critical.

At the same time, there are some general concepts and ideas that we can draw from that come together to make up strategies that tend to help most children with AS. They are flexible strategies that can be incorporated in different ways. No intervention or treatment solves the underlying cause of ASD.

Education should begin early, as soon as they are identified as having autism. The earlier education start, the more possible it is to avoid some of the challenges that the child will experience. Early identification is a great help to bolstering the child's development. The programming must be individualized for each child. These goals should be based on the child's developmental level and pattern of skills and strengths, as well as the parent's judgment about what is important. Each child will have different learning patterns. Goals and objectives need to be reviewed and reevaluated with frequency. Large groups of classes for kids with ASD are rarely effective because of the unique individual needs of each child. One-to-one teaching is often necessary. Once these skills are learned, they can be practiced and maintained in larger group settings.

The teaching should help the child to address their learning pattern. Parents and teachers should look to increase the patterns that lend themselves to healthy development and help the child notice and decrease patterns that lead them toward more negative behaviors. Much of the early teaching will involve social and communication skills. These are the biggest problem areas for kids with ASD and need to be identified for each child based on his or her needs and strengths. This can be bolstered by responding to other's facial expressions and nonverbal gestures, imitating others, language use, and play.

One prominent educational model for children with ASD is Applied Behavior Analysis. This involves training sessions, in which a caregiver or therapist asks a child with AS to do or say certain things and reinforces the response that comes close to the request. There is a separate challenge with each request, and it becomes a separate opportunity to learn. As the child is rewarded for the appropriate responses, they begin to learn to interact in this way and become more reinforced in communication. This can be used to teach skills in all domains of life, including daily activities of self-care, social interaction and emotional understanding. Each thing that is being taught, no matter how complicated, gets broken down into smaller goals.

This is the process of making the child available to have successes. The shaping of behavior results in a modification toward more positive behavior. There are some strong advocates for the ABA approach who recommend 40 hours per week of training with the child, for several years. This may not be attainable or practical for most families, but even so, consistent, structured, intensive, repetitive, and focused teaching tends to be effective in building skills in children with ASD.

The ABA program is designed to be implemented in a classroom setting with other children with ASD or in the child's home, where one-to-one teaching is not interrupted.

Chapter 8: Mental Health Management

Undoubtedly, living in the normatively-based society that we do, a child will face emotional struggles from time to time. They may be based on frustrations around functioning or relating to other people, they may come from social isolation, or the child may just be feeling everyday stress like all of us to from time to time. We can help children with ASD grow their awareness of feelings and learn to deal with them. Strong feelings will be more difficult to deal with, but all can be handled in a helpful way. First, the child should be able to label and identify their feelings. This will allow them to discuss their emotions and feelings. They must also learn to be able to use feelings as a tool in social interaction. Some children will have trouble expressing their feelings, and find difficulty in measured signals involving their feelings. Often, children will express them as catastrophic and overwhelming events.

Obsessive behaviors can come in here like biting, hitting, or becoming self-absorbed. Once the child is able to modify their response to be less extreme, they can signal their feelings in a helpful way. Once the child masters this stage, they can move on to the next stage, which is applying words, symbols, and pretend sequence to the feeling during play. Dolls can hit or hug each other; the mommy doll can ask the baby doll questions. The child will see how these adult-guided interactions work and learn new ways of expressing and coping with the feeling.

Adults should try to feel free to act out feelings, even feelings like anger or aggression, in playtime, in order to be able to model and appropriate expression of anger. If you don't help the child to use imagination to express the feeling, they are left with no outlet to express. This will result in tension, anxiety, and compulsiveness.

Anxiety can sometimes become a problem for children with ASD, particularly those who are more sensitive to sensory stimulation. They become anxious and fearful and always are thinking about the worst things that can happen. They get easily overloaded by their won awareness and are very reactive to their own n emotions. To begin helping children with this pattern of mental struggle, parents and caregivers should help the child learn to relax. Breathing exercises can be very helpful for this. Self-calming and self-soothing are important so that the child learns to relax and be able to sooth itself.

The more anxious and scared the child is, the more comforting the parents and the environment should be. If the child is verbal, ask for their input. Ask about plans for tomorrow, or ways that they can make the day more enjoyable. Thinking about the plans for tomorrow can be a very useful technique to get kids to think about the big picture. Children who worry easily are often less comfortable with expressing feelings of anger. They are scared of the anger. You can help them to become more comfortable with these feelings by talking about situations that annoy or challenge them. If they are having trouble in school and the child thins the teach was being unfair, you should ask about what the child is feeling, and how they would set up the classroom if they had the choice.

The fear of anger is not the only aversion to expressing feeling that children with ASD have. They might also be scared of their feelings, like sadness, because their feelings overwhelm them and then they feel shame at the face of feeling out of control. In this situation, parents and caregivers have a chance to make the child feel accepted for their feelings. The parent must remain engaged, soothing, and accepting. The child will learn to let down their defenses a little bit more. Then, the child can be encouraged to go into more detail about their feelings, through conversation or play.

If the child says, "I don't want to cry," you can ask "Really? What does that feel like" It be hard to stop crying when your body wants to cry." This is showing empathy with the child's ability y to contain the feeling and help them describe the conflict.

As a child deals with this level of development, they need to become comfortable with assertiveness. Many children who say they don't want to cry haven't gotten comfortable with this side of them, which involves expressing and coping with aggression and anger. The child must learn to participate in actions that are constructive, getting ideas an asserting them.

Emotional range and balance are two abilities that a child must develop for healthy functioning. They are not always easy to achieve together. When adults are said to be healthy, we usually handle people who are able to show a broad range of emotion and can regulate their emotions and come back to equilibrium if they get upset. They are supposed to be "balanced." Parents and caregivers can support emotional range and balance in children with ASD.

One of the most important parts of dealing with mental health, especially with this population, is acceptance. Don't assume that positive emotions are good and other emotions are bad; this will make the child's expression very constricted. We need to strive to accept all of the emotions equally. A toddler may be experimenting with assertiveness; enjoy that assertive interaction and work with the child. If they're pointing to a toy on the shelf and trying to get up and get it, do not tell them no. Rather, you can ask them "how can I help you?" interacting with the child in this way encourages her to signal to you with communication that she wants to be picked up. This way, she learns that assertiveness can become a safe, collaborative effort, rather than a rebellion. Accept the emotion, and then engage with it.

Next is to provide structure and guidance so that the child doesn't get overwhelmed by the experience of the emotion. Engaging in the emotion shouldn't overstimulate or scare the child when the adult is involved. It should be regulated with reasonable limits. If you help the child reach the toy in a safe and secure way, the child will be able to do something that is beyond their limit but achieve it safely.

Chapter 9: Visual Tools

Research has shown that visual tools and supports are great for learning in early development for children with ASD. A visual support refers to a picture or other visual tool that helps communication with the child. This helps to make up for the deficit in language so that the child can look at a photograph, drawing, or object, derive meaning from them, and use them for communication. These visual tools help the child to communicate with their parents and also with other members of their family or community. Visual supports are used with children with ASD, but can also be used in the lives of people with ASD of all ages. Visual tools may be used by teachers, doctors, caregivers, and therapists.

Visual tools are important because some of the main challenges that are associated with autism and Autism Spectrum Disorder involve interacting and using language. Children with ASD might not understand social cues when interacting with others.

They might not have a good idea of how to start a conversation, or how to act when others approach them. They might be missing out on when to use their social skills. These problems with social skills can also make it difficult for children with ASD to follow spoken instructions. Visuals can help the child express what they want and it can help caregivers express what they want out of the child. Better communication decreases frustration and can help decrease obsessive behaviors. Visual tools are appropriate, positive ways to communicate.

Visual tools can help children understand what to expect and what will happen next, reducing their anxiety. Visual tools can help them pay attention to important details and help them cope with change.

One example of a visual tool is the "First-Then Board." This is a visual display of something that is rewarding, which will happen after a task is completed. The "First-Then Board" will show a picture of the desired behavior. This might be something like "eating lunch" or "washing your hair." Then the board will show a picture of the reward, which could be anything from playground time to dessert. This helps the child to follow directions and learn new skills. This helps with motivations to do activities that they don't like and makes clear when they can do the fun stuff. It also helps with language, incorporating visual-logical processing into the day.

Another example of a visual tool would be a visual schedule. A visual schedule is a representation of what's going to happen for any particular day. The schedule could include breakfast, school, therapy, outside time, or any number of activities. It is helpful for decreasing anxiety in children and decreasing rigidity. Another area that the visual schedule helps with is sequencing. As the child learns the basics of sequencing, you can encourage them to think in higher levels of complex sequencing over time.

Visual tools are part of a category of learning that involves sensory stimulation. Other parts of this category include music, art, and exercise. Music can be a great way to communicate information, just like visual tools. Music can function in a way where the child is empowered to express their feelings. It can also help to bolster appropriate interaction with others. When a child learns to clap along with a pulse with other children and adults, they are learning to be cohesive in a group and enact their role in support of others. Another sense area that can be great for work with art and music is the tactile sense. Children can use motor skills in activities like grasping a drum mallet or painting. Finger painting can combine visual-logical reasoning and tactile sensation. Musical instruments like drums and keyboards do this well. The emotional content in the art or music can help the child to connect ideas. If they learn how to paint what happy looks like, or play what happy sounds like, they come closer to being able to identify emotions, which is a very important skill. This will help with emotional regulation and relating to others.

Chapter 10: Play Time and Physical Exercise

As we mentioned earlier, playtime is very important for children learning to build bridges between concepts, feelings, language, and ideas. Play can help children to connect the abstract with reality. This may manifest as a newfound understanding of emotion after acting out an emotional scene, or a greater idea of why it is important to be on time.

At the foundation of this endeavor is trust. The parent or whoever else is working with the child must provide a protective, stable, and supportive relationship. This foundation includes the child's sense that they are physically safe and that they can have a sense of security. Some families are pretty natural at providing this; others require a great deal of support or therapy in order to learn how to do this. Poverty and other circumstances outside of the family's control can lead to the absence of the conditions required to build a safe relationship.

Psychiatrists, psychologists, and social workers may be able to help families who don't have a secure environment to establish one. This secure environment, if established can lead to an ongoing and consistent relationship. Every child requires a consistent and ongoing relationship in order to develop cognitively and grow healthily. Children with ASD often have difficulty relating and will require warm, consistent caregiving. Sometimes it is difficult for caregivers to sustain the intimate relationships. Parents may have trouble perceiving their child's intentions accurately.

Understanding problematic behavior is necessary to help caregivers move past the misperceptions and move on the better ways of relating to the parent. One example is touch. Children may be very sensitive to touch early on, and they may reject the parents attempt to touch them. This can be hard for a parent to take. It may be important to avoid light touch at first and to use deep pressure to make them feel more comfortable. This can be somewhat unintuitive, as parents might not understand the subtlety of why this works.

In the secure environment that has been established, a parent can work to engage in play with the child to help them increases their social and learning interactions. Often times, the most effective way to establish communication is to get down onto the floor with the child. The time spent on the floor allows the child to take the lead and design interactions that fit their unique needs. There are six fundamental skills that are being fostered when a parent engages in play with the child: attention, relation, communication, problem-solving, creativity, and logical ruse of ideas. You can start at the bottom of the ladder and keep working up until the child learns to use ideas logically. This is done with reelection and with creativity.

Once a child starts becoming comfortable in interacting with one person and establishes a two-way communication with an adult. Parents can try out group play dates with peers. The child must learn to communicate with her peers as well. This process is helped along if peer groups are initiated early in life. If the child waits until they are older to join groups, they may find it harder to learn and relate spontaneously. The goal here is to aid children's ability to be near others and exist in their presence, to communicate, and to just be with others in general. Peer play is very important when children are starting to use ideas intentionally and at-will. They will need to see what happens when they use their new skills not only with the people they are used to but also other children that are at the same or a higher level of development in somewhat. They don't need to be the same age; children of varying ages are at various stages of development, and a four-year-old may enjoy the company of a three-year-old.

Problem-solving interactions are big in play; they can engage the child in all sorts of ways, including motor, sensory, and visual-spatial. These interactions, if enacted well, can get the child involved with emotions but also improve speech, processing abilities, and language skills. The adult takes the lead, guiding the child through the problem and how to solve it. They become a model of behavior for the child. Sometimes a child will want to investigate an object or toy, rather than just playing with it. They may try to feel all over the teddy bear to explore its shape or look specifically at certain parts of a toy. Parents and caregivers can help kids in this stage by helping them to explore. Other times, kids will engage in cause-and-effect play. This is when they learn that if they carry out a certain action, they will get a certain result. This can help to increase childrens' sense of reality orientation and expectations. Another category of play is "functional" play. This is when the child uses toys in the expected way for which they were designed.

So why use play to try to accomplish all of these seemingly complicated goals? The answer is that it works. Play is the way that children relate to the world. This makes it a great environment to learn and develop. Play can be highly individualized for each child. One child will use a toy in a completely different way than another, and they will have different reasons for liking it. It is in these differences that we can learn about the child.

Constructive play is a certain type of play, wherein children build things or create things. It might involve working towards a single product, for example completing a puzzle, or drawing a picture. This can be an area of difficulty for children with ASD and adults should try to help them along. You can encourage constructive play by showing your child what to do with the building blocks.

Physical play is "rough-and-tumble" play. It includes running around and other full body exercises. Physical play involves a lot of physical sensation, which can engage the child but can also over stimulate the child. Physical play is great for developing gross motor skills. It also gives children a chance to feel out their environment.

Pretend play is where children pretend to enact a "scene" and use their imagination. Types of pretend play could include pretending to feed a doll, dressing up like a movie character, pretending to drive a car, or pretending the floor is lava. This usually happens later on in a child's development, around two years in. It is considered a sophisticated form of play, in that it engages creativity and cognitive skills more than other forms of play. It can be very helpful in developing language skills and social skills. This type of play can be delayed in development for children with ASD, but many do develop it. There are many every-day activities that can be helped by pretend play. Once a child is doing pretend actions, a parent or caregiver can provide more specific structure for the action, and increase desirable behaviors. Role-playing is a big part of pretend play. Parents and caregivers should encourage role-playing in children with ASD.

You might be able to tell them a story and have them act it out. By introducing relevant and healthy themes in the story, the child will learn the values and problem solving that the story entails.

Parents and caregivers should strive to provide environments where children can have social play to develop their social skills. This very important ability – the ability to play with others – can help alleviate social stress and increase social skills. First, notice what stage of social play the child is at, and provide appropriate and safe opportunities to get to the next stage.

The first stage is playing alone. This is when the child plays alone and independently. They don't pay much attention to the other children and don't try to involve them in their play. The next stage is parallel play. This is where children start to play alongside other children. They might share some toys or interact, but at a basic level, they are connecting by being "alongside." Identifying what the child enjoys and helping them to play with other kids who enjoy the same toys can help this stage along. The next stage is associative play. This is where children are playing and sharing with others. They are giving and taking, learning to share and meet their needs. This usually starts around three years. Next comes cooperative play. This is when the child is playing with others, and cooperating with rules or even making up rules.

Cooperative play can become very complicated and involves communication skills. Sometimes the social rules that are involved in this type of play are difficult for children with ASD. Once the child has learned to develop through these stages, you can help them to cultivate relationships with others. Simple games are a nice way to build social interaction in play. Turn-taking skills and attention skills are grown by engaging in games and play with others.

Play skills can be transferred to life skills. Turn-taking done appropriately should be rewarded in play. This is an example of a play skill that is very useful in everyday life.

Experiences like jumping on a trampoline, running, or throwing a ball around, can be very beneficial for motor, sensory and spatial skills. Physical activities that engender even more creativity include obstacle courses and games such as treasure hunts.

Exercise can be a fantastic way to increase positive behavior in kids with ASD. Research studies have shown that an increase in exercise can lead to improvements in children with ASD in several areas. Among these is behavior regulation, where a child learns through sport or physical activity to regulate their behavior and keep it appropriate to the rules and boundaries of the game. Another is school readiness.

Exercise and sports can help a child in this area by preparing them for active group participation and completion of tasks. Academic engagement can be increased, by increasing attention span and cognitive skills. Motor skills, of course, are also increased, as the child learns how to use their body for the tasks involved in exercise. Many children with ASD have non-typical patterns of physical activity or non-typical dietary patterns, so exercise can help maintain a healthy body if it is consistent and gentle. Becoming overweight or having other problems due to inactivity can lead children with ASD toward emotional problems, depression, anxiety, or gastrointestinal problems. Children with ASD are also found to usually have a lower bone density than their peers, so exercise can help strengthen their systems and make negative outcomes more avoidable.

The amount of exercise that a child with ASD needs is not excessive; sometimes, a vigorous activity for just one minute, whether it is jumping jacks, pushups, or running in place, can help reduce disruptive and off-task behaviors.

The best way to distribute exercise activities may be to give students small breaks throughout the day. This can help correct responding and on-task behavior in kids with ASD. Vigorous exercise will have more impact than less strenuous activity, but this must be tempered by making sure that the child is not feeling overstressed or required to do more than they can handle.

As the child grows and has more opportunities to participate in group sports, they will find themselves having to navigate the difficulties of how their social skills impact their ability to be part of the team. Some students will find themselves inhibited when trying to become part of the team. However, if there is an interest in the child for a particular sport or activity, it should be encouraged, and often, an inclusive program will be able to involve the child can build fitness, social skills, and connections. These types of connections that happen in sports-based interaction can have very positive life-long benefits. Sometimes track and cross-country can be a good fit for adolescents with ASD.

Martial arts, dance, or other equestrian programs are great options. It can be helpful when a child is going to be involved in exercise routines to create a weekly calendar with built-in time slot for exercise. You can increase the amount over time, and make a note of activities that might need transportation, special clothing, or equipment. These logistics are sometimes difficult when children are having trouble with activities of daily living. You can use an app or another reminder to prompt yourself or the child when the time is near to exercise. You can also use technology to track accomplishments and progress. A positive reward system can be a really great way to make sure the child is seeing a reason to exercise in the initial stages of the exercise routine. After a while, if a child successfully maintains an exercise routine, endorphins and naturally feeling good will become the reward.

Chapter 11: Relating with Family, Siblings, and Others

All families will experience different dynamics when they receive a diagnosis of ASD in a child. The family will need to adapt to meet the unforeseen needs of the child and reconfigure the support system of the family. Oftentimes, mothers are the ones who assume a large part of the care for the child. As a result of this, fathers sometimes take on a bigger responsibility for the financial requirements of the family. These are decisions that made about dividing the family workload. Ideally, families would be able to take everyone's needs and abilities into account, but unfortunately, it doesn't always end up that way. Often, the decision about roles in the family is made on the grounds of practicality, in response to immediate demands.

The two partners I the caregiver roles may become uncomfortably separate, leading them to feel unsupported by the other. Exhaustion can follow if one parent is responsible for the majority of the care and interventions for the child. The parents who are responsible for the family's financial position may take on great extra stress as well. Parents will need to sot out their roles to the best of their abilities and make sure to try to prevent burnout.

Raising a child with ASD can be a challenge, and it takes some adjustment and sacrifice on the part of all of the family members. Some crises come up, and the family must get through them. Parents may feel overwhelmed at times. Each family member will have his or her own way of dealing with stress. Some people need to express their emotions more readily than others. Some people feel that the issues surrounding the care of a child with ASD are private and should be kept that way. Others will seek input and support from family and friends. Yoga, meditation, massage, and other forms of self-care can relieve stress.

Each role in the family will have a different relationship with the child with ASD. Whoever is the primary caretaker for the child will have a certain type of relationship. The parent who is seen less will be held in a slightly different regard. Extended members of the family, depending on their proximity and type of role in the family, can be great role models and supporters for children with ASD.

Sibling relationship can be the longest lasting family bonds for any person. There is a high variability, however, in how siblings get along with each other.

Sometimes siblings will be close as children and their relationships will fall off as adults. Some others will never have closeness until adulthood. In any case, siblings can be a great source of happiness and connection. Siblings have widely varying interests, personalities, and values. Parents with a child with ASD cannot assume that any one thing will happen in the sibling relationships. It is largely outside of their control. They can, however, establish a family environment that engenders respect and caring and an environment like this teaches kids about relationships in general and family responsibilities.

Parents should work not to neglect the needs of their children without ASD when the one with it comes along. They can help all of their children understand ASD so that they can have some context for their sibling's personality and behavior. Young children may have to have ASD explained to them, to match their level of understanding. Preschoolers might accept an explanation like "Mike doesn't enjoy when there's a lot of noise. It makes him feel bad." As children grow, they start to see the differences in their own responses to those of the child with ASD. This might require further explanation. As they grow into the level where they are able to understand more about ASD, they can be encouraged to read about ASD from a responsible source. Then, parents can discuss with their children what they learned. At every stage, parents will need to take the lead in bringing up the topic. It is a complex subject, and sometimes children have trouble thinking of the right questions to ask. They may feel that the topic is off-limits. Siblings may also feel that they cannot express their emotion toward the child with ASD. Parents who are open with their children will find that openness can bring a sense of contentment and understanding.

Extended family members may experience a shift in the family dynamics as well. The term ASD may be very confusing to grandparents, for example. If the child is generally high functioning, older family members may be skeptical of the family's decision to seek a diagnosis. Most young parents in our current are more tuned into the realities of learning, development, and intellectual disorders. Inclusion for people with disabilities is fairly common in some communities now.

Disability is stigmatized less than ever in some places. In other cultures and areas, it is still seen as a mark of shame. If older family memes were raised in an environment which shamed disability, they might have internalized that message early on. Some education will be necessary for folks who have this viewpoint. The parents will need to decide how much education lies in their responsibility and where to draw boundaries between explaining and leaving it alone. When explaining about ASD to family members who display ignorance of the subject, try to nicely explain why the disorder is outside of the family's control, part of the child's unique makeup as a person, and politely explain that you accept and love the child for who they are.

Close friends are a huge part of human life and are important for self-esteem and safe outlets of expression. Friends can be trusted not to share secrets. Making friends will be a journey for a child with ASD; as they move through various levels of development, they will meet others who share similar characteristics. As they share more and more experiences with other children, parents should look to help along friendships. Parents themselves often find themselves lacking friendships.

Conclusion

Thank you for making it through to the end of *Autism – Parent Guide to Autism Spectrum Disorder*, let's hope it was informative and able to provide you with all of the tools you need to achieve your goals whatever they may be.

In this book, we've looked at the contemporary understanding of Autism Spectrum Disorder and its characteristics. This understanding lets us see a path to know how we can comprehend a child's interaction, sensory experiences, and thinking patterns. It may seem difficult to sort through all the available information on this subject, and there are lots of other sources out there that have lots of good information on Autism Spectrum Disorder. This book can provide a foundation to think about the disorder and understand the challenges and ways to face problems when raising a child with ASD. We should now be far from the old conception of ASD, which likened children to out-of-control maniacs who couldn't be taught or interacted with. ASD has now become a nationally understood phenomenon.

Families can have full, joyous, excellent lives with their child with ASD. The family's perspective is really important. If the family lives with the disorder in the dark and never processes it within the family, they will find more problems in the relationships in the family. If they find a way to celebrate the uniqueness of their child and incorporate the child into the family community successfully, they will find that their lives improve immensely. Kids with ASD are totally capable of building relationships and being excellent friends, children, and students.

Parents will most likely face challenges in their journey raising a child with ASD. However, they should work to see the beauty and uniqueness in their child's spirit. The first stages of parenting a child with ASD come along with a response to immediate needs.

Finding schools, finding ways for the child to adapt to in-the-moment problems becomes the primary mode. It takes a lot of planning and a lot of collaboration. Parents might want to examine their ability to collaborate with others and try to maximize their ability in this area. As life goes on, it will settle into routine and rhythm. Parents will undoubtedly make mistakes; the important thing is that they strive to understand their child so that they can adapt along with the child and help them to achieve to the highest level. Indeed, a parent's journey in this path will often lead to a process of development that they themselves must attempt. These challenges, however, ultimately serve to enrich the lives of the parent, as they learn a deeper humanity and connection than they could've thought possible. There is a special magic when a connection can be made with a child with ASD.

Once you've read this book, the next step is to look at some other sources and compare them with observations of the child. All of the information that parents take in at the crucial early stages of parenting a child with ASD can help the parents to be adjusted, helpful, and cognizant of issues that come up.

BONUS:

As a way of saying thank you for purchasing my book, please use your link below to claim your free ebook

I have laid down Top 10 Tips Guide for you to Overcoming Obsessions and Compulsions Using Mindfulness

https://bit.ly/2TDMNkn

You can also share your link with your friends and families whom you think that can benefit from the guide or you can forward them the link as a gift!